Imagine! **1**

Rainforest Rescue

By Paul Shipton

Illustrated by Fabiano Fiorin

Activities by Hannah Fish

D0784171

Contents

OXFORD

UNIVERSITY PRESS

Ben
Rosie's brother

Rosie
Ben's sister

Grandpa

Clunk
Grandpa's robot

Alice
Rosie's friend

Now let's read this story, Rainforest Rescue!

'I'm hungry,' says Grandpa. 'What fruit do we have?'

'We have apples and bananas,' says Clunk. 'Here you are.'

'No, thank you,' says Grandpa. 'I want to eat my favorite fruit today!'

I'm hungry.

Rosie is in the kitchen with her friend, Alice.

'What's your favorite fruit, Grandpa?' asks Rosie.

Grandpa walks to the door. 'We can go and find it! Come with me!'

'Can I come, too?' asks Ben.

Can I come, too?

Go to page 20 for activities.

In the van, Grandpa says to Clunk, 'Let's go!'

'Where, Grandpa?' asks Ben. 'Do you want to go to the store?'

'No!' says Grandpa.

Clunk starts the van and drives.

The van stops in a new place. It's hot here.

The children look at the trees and plants.

'Where are we?' asks Rosie.

'We're in a rainforest!' says Ben.

'My favorite fruit is the durian,' says Grandpa. 'We can find it in this rainforest.'

He and the children walk in the rainforest and look for a durian.

Grandpa points up. 'There!' he says. 'I can see some durians in that tree!'

'I can climb up and get some durians,' says Ben.

'Clunk, go up the tree too, please,' says Grandpa.

Then the girls hear a noise.

'What's that?' asks Alice.

What's that?

→ Go to page 22 for activities.

There's a cage next to a tree. And there's an animal in the cage!

'What's that?' asks Rosie.

'It's a baby orangutan,' says Grandpa. He's angry. 'Some people take animals from the rainforest. They can sell young orangutans.'

It's a baby orangutan.

Grandpa opens the cage.

Soon the orangutan is in Alice's arms. 'Don't be scared,' she says.

'He wants his mother,' says Rosie.

'Baby orangutans live with their mothers for years,' says Grandpa.

He wants his mother.

Go to page 23 for activities.

Two men walk out of the trees.

'That's our orangutan!' shouts the tall man. 'Give him to us!'

'No,' says Alice. 'You can't take him out of the rainforest. It's his home.'

That's our orangutan!

The men are angry.

'We want that orangutan and you can't stop us!' shouts one man.

The two men run at Grandpa and the girls.

→ Go to page 24 for activities.

Then a big durian falls from the tree!
It hits the ground close to the men.

'What's that?' shouts the tall man.

'I can smell it!' says his friend. 'It
smells very bad!'

What's that?

Then two, three, four ... a lot of durians hit the ground.

'Run!' shouts the tall man.

In the tree, Ben has a durian in his hand.

'We can stop now,' he says to Clunk.

We can stop now.

Go to page 25 for activities.

'But what about the baby orangutan?' asks Alice.

Rosie points and says, 'Look. The mother orangutan is there.'

The big orangutan is angry.

'She wants her baby,' says Grandpa.

Rosie is scared. 'What can we do?' she asks.

Alice knows. She puts the baby orangutan on the ground.

'Here,' she says to the big orangutan.

With her long arms, the mother takes her baby.

Go to page 26 for activities.

The orangutan climbs up a tree with her baby.

'They're happy now,' says Alice.

Ben and Clunk climb down from the tree.

'Here's your fruit, Grandpa,' says Ben.

Here's your fruit, Grandpa.

Grandpa opens the fruit.

Rosie puts her hand on her nose. 'I can smell it!' she says.

'I love durians,' says Grandpa. 'But they smell very bad!'

→ Go to page 27 for activities.

Activities for pages 4–5

1 Put a tick (✓) or a cross (✗) in the box.

1 This is fruit. ✓

2 This is a kitchen. ☐

3 This is an apple. ☐

4 This is a banana. ☐

2 Write *yes* or *no*.

1 Grandpa is hungry. _yes_

2 They have apples and bananas. _____

3 Grandpa wants to eat a banana. _____

4 Grandpa wants to eat his
  favorite fruit. _____

5 Rosie and Alice are in the kitchen. _____

6 Clunk says, 'Can I come, too?' _____

Talk What's your favorite fruit? Talk to a friend.

Activities for pages 6-7

1 Circle the correct words.

1 'Do you want **going** / **to go** to the store?'
2 Clunk **starts** / **start** the van and drives.
3 The van stops **in** / **on** a new place.
4 The new place **are** / **is** hot.
5 The children **see** / **look at** the trees.
6 They are **in** / **at** a rainforest.

2 Write the words.

1 n a v

van

2 e e r t

_____

3 l t a n p s

_____

4 t s r o e

_____

5 e s t a i r n f r o

_____

6 c e p a l

_____

Activities for pages 8–9

1 Choose and write the correct words.

Grandpa's favorite fruit is the ¹ ___durian___ .
Grandpa and the children walk in the rainforest.
They ² _____ a durian. Grandpa sees some
durians in a tree. Ben says, 'I can ³ _____ up
and get some.' Then the girls hear a ⁴ _____.

climb   fruit   ~~durian~~   noise   look for

2 Match.

1 Grandpa and the children   and get some durians.

2 Grandpa can see   hear a noise.

3 Ben can climb up   look for durians.

4 Rosie and Alice   'What's that?'

5 Alice says,   some durians in a tree.

Talk **What is the noise? Tell a friend your ideas.**

Activities for pages 10–11

1 Order the words.

1 animal / in a / There's / cage. / an

There's an animal in a cage.

2 baby orangutan. / a / The / is / animal

_____

3 take / rainforest. / animals / Some people / from the

_____

4 opens / cage. / Grandpa / the

_____

5 is in / Soon / Alice's / the orangutan / arms.

_____

2 Look at the picture on page 10. Answer the questions.

1 How many girls are there? _two_

2 How many orangutans are there? _____

3 Where is the baby orangutan? in a _____

4 Where is the cage? _____ a tree

Activities for pages 12–13

1 Complete the sentences.

> take   stop   ~~walk~~   run   are

1 Two men ___walk___ out of the trees.

2 Alice says, 'You can't _____ him out of the rainforest.'

3 The men _____ angry.

4 One man shouts, 'We want that orangutan and you can't _____ us!'

5 The men _____ at Grandpa and the girls.

2 Write *yes* or *no*.

1 Three men walk out of the trees.   _____

2 The men want the orangutan.   _____

3 The rainforest is the orangutan's home.   _____

4 The men are angry.   _____

5 Grandpa runs at the men.   _____

Talk Do the men take the baby orangutan? Tell a friend your ideas.

24

1 Write the words.

1 u n r

_____

2 o u r g n d

_____

3 i t h

_____

4 m e l s l

_____

5 l l a f

_____

6 a n d h

_____

2 Match.

1 The durian	shouts, 'Run!'
2 A lot of durians	'We can stop now.'
3 The tall man	a durian in his hand.
4 Ben has	hit the ground.
5 Ben says,	smells very bad.

Activities for pages 16–17

1 Choose and write the correct words.

The mother orangutan is ¹ _____.

She wants her baby. Rosie is ² _____.

Alice puts the baby ³ _____ on the

ground. The mother takes her ⁴ _____

with her long arms.

scared   baby   ground   orangutan   angry

2 Look at the picture on page 16. Answer the questions.

1 How many orangutans are there? _____

2 Where is the baby orangutan?

in Alice's _____

3 What is Grandpa looking at?

the mother _____

4 Is the mother orangutan angry? _____

5 What color is the mother orangutan? _____

Activities for pages 18–19

1 Circle the correct words.

1 The mother orangutan climbs **up** / **down** a tree.

2 The orangutans **is** / **are** happy now.

3 Ben gives Grandpa **a** / **an** durian.

4 Grandpa opens **the** / **it** fruit.

5 Rosie puts her hand **at** / **on** her nose.

6 Durians **smell** / **are smelling** bad.

2 Put a tick (✓) or a cross (✗) in the box.

1 This is a tree. ☐

2 This is a durian. ☐

3 This is a hand. ☐

4 This is a nose. ☐

Talk **Do you like this story? Talk to a friend.**

Rainforest Animals

1 **Draw a picture of orangutans. Then read about them.**

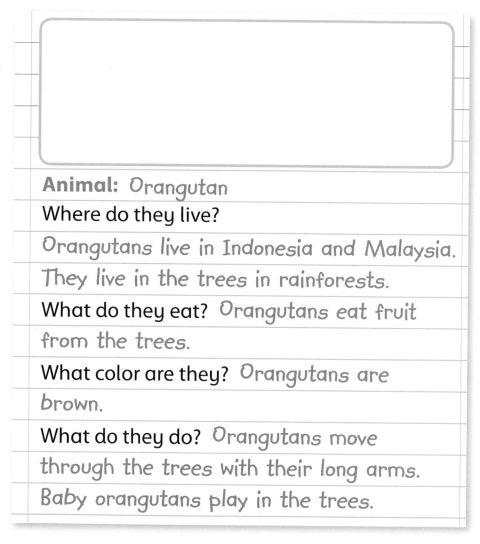

Animal: Orangutan

Where do they live?

Orangutans live in Indonesia and Malaysia. They live in the trees in rainforests.

What do they eat? Orangutans eat fruit from the trees.

What color are they? Orangutans are brown.

What do they do? Orangutans move through the trees with their long arms. Baby orangutans play in the trees.

Talk **Do you know more about orangutans? Talk to a friend.**

2 **Find out about two more rainforest animals. Draw them and answer the questions.**

Animal:

Where do they live?

What do they eat?

What color are they?

What do they do?

Animal:

Where do they live?

What do they eat?

What color are they?

What do they do?

Talk **Talk to a friend about your rainforest animals.**

angry

animals

apple

baby

banana

cage

climb

down

durian

fall

fruit

ground

hand

hit

hot

kitchen

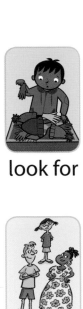 look for

 noise

 nose

orangutan

 people

 place

 plants

 rainforest

 scared

 sell

 shout

 smell

 store

 tree

 up

 van

Oxford Read and Imagine

Oxford Read and Imagine graded readers are at nine levels (Early Starter, Starter, Beginner, and Levels 1 to 6) for students from age 3 or 4 and older. They offer great stories to read and enjoy.

Activities provide Cambridge Young Learner Exams preparation. See Key below.

At Levels 1 to 6, every storybook reader links to an **Oxford Read and Discover** non-fiction reader, giving students a chance to find out more about the world around them, and an opportunity for Content and Language Integrated Learning (CLIL).

For more information about **Read and Imagine**, and for Teacher's Notes, go to www.oup.com/elt/teacher/readandimagine

KEY Activity supports Cambridge Young Learners Starters Exam preparation

Oxford Read and Discover

What's your favorite fruit? Do you want to learn about different fruit? You can read this non-fiction book.

OXFORD
UNIVERSITY PRESS

Great Clarendon Street, Oxford, OX2 6DP, United Kingdom

Oxford University Press is a department of the University of Oxford. It furthers the University's objective of excellence in research, scholarship, and education by publishing worldwide. Oxford is a registered trade mark of Oxford University Press in the UK and in certain other countries

No unauthorized photocopying

ISBN: 978 0 19 472269 8

Printed in China

This book is printed on paper from certified and well-managed sources

ACKNOWLEDGEMENTS

Main illustrations by: Fabiano Fiorin/Milan Illustrations Agency.

Activity illustrations by: Dusan Pavlic/Beehive Illustration, Alan Rowe, Mark Ruffle.